# MANNERS
# AT SCHOOL

## JOSH PLATTNER

Consulting Editor, Diane Craig, M.A./Reading Specialist

**Sandcastle**

An Imprint of Abdo Publishing
abdopublishing.com

# abdopublishing.com

Published by Abdo Publishing, a division of ABDO, PO Box 398166, Minneapolis, Minnesota 55439. Copyright © 2016 by Abdo Consulting Group, Inc. International copyrights reserved in all countries. No part of this book may be reproduced in any form without written permission from the publisher. SandCastle™ is a trademark and logo of Abdo Publishing.

Printed in the United States of America, North Mankato, Minnesota

062015
092015

**THIS BOOK CONTAINS RECYCLED MATERIALS**

Editor: Alex Kuskowski
Content Developer: Nancy Tuminelly
Cover and Interior Design and Production: Mighty Media, Inc.
Photo Credits: Shutterstock

**Library of Congress Cataloging-in-Publication Data**

Plattner, Josh.

Manners at school / Josh Plattner ; consulting editor, Diane Craig, M.A., Reading Specialist.

pages cm. -- (Manners)

Audience: PreK to grade 3.

ISBN 978-1-62403-716-0

1. Student etiquette. I. Title.

BJ1857.C5S87 2016

395.5--dc23

2014046545

## SandCastle™ Level: Transitional

SandCastle™ books are created by a team of professional educators, reading specialists, and content developers around five essential components—phonemic awareness, phonics, vocabulary, text comprehension, and fluency—to assist young readers as they develop reading skills and strategies and increase their general knowledge. All books are written, reviewed, and leveled for guided reading, early reading intervention, and Accelerated Reader® programs for use in shared, guided, and independent reading and writing activities to support a balanced approach to literacy instruction. The SandCastle™ series has four levels that correspond to early literacy development. The levels are provided to help teachers and parents select appropriate books for young readers.

EMERGING · BEGINNING · **TRANSITIONAL** · FLUENT

# CONTENTS

# MANNERS AT SCHOOL

Good manners are great!
They make school fun.
They help you learn.

# BUS BASICS

Ann rides the bus.

She stays in her seat.

She keeps her hands
to herself.

# RIDING ALONG

Mac is on a field trip.

He does not yell.

He shares his bus seat.

# IN THE HALL

Be **polite** in the hall. Give others space. Do not run. Use your **indoor** voice.

# CLASSROOM CARE

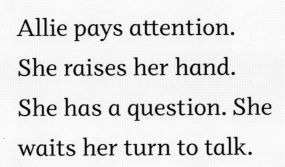

Allie pays attention.
She raises her hand.
She has a question. She
waits her turn to talk.

# CLEAN-UP TIME

Don't leave toys on the ground at recess. Take the time to clean up! Put toys back where they belong.

# SUPER SHARING

Dan shares colored pencils with his **classmates**. Everyone takes turns using them. They have fun drawing together.

# SUPER SUBJECTS

Try your best to learn
new things. Try even if
the subject is not your
favorite. It shows respect.

# FRIEND CENTER

Make friends at school! Smile at your **classmates**. Be **polite**. Everyone you meet at school could be a new friend.

# KEEP IT UP!

Always practice good manners at school. Can you think of more? What else could you do?

# GLOSSARY

**classmate** – a student who is in the same class as you.

**indoor** – inside a building.

**polite** – having good manners or showing consideration for others.